Brighter Grammar 2

An English Grammar with Exercises
New edition

C E Eckersley
Margaret Macaulay
Revised by D K Swan

Longman

Longman Group UK Limited,
Longman House, Burnt Mill, Harlow,
Essex CM20 2JE, England
and Associated Companies throughout the world.

© Longman Group UK Limited 1952, 1987

First published 1952
Seventh impression 1990

ISBN 0-582-55896-4

Set in 10/12 pt Linotron Times
Produced by Longman Singapore Publishers Pte Ltd
Printed in Singapore

Contents

(Each lesson is followed by exercises)

Lesson One

Parts of speech

Revision. There are eight parts of speech: **nouns** (names of anything), **pronouns** (words standing instead of nouns), **adjectives** (words limiting the meaning of nouns), **verbs** (words expressing an action or state of being), **adverbs** (words limiting the meaning of verbs), **conjunctions** (joining words), **prepositions** (words used with nouns or pronouns to make phrases), **interjections** (words used to express a sudden feeling).

If you are asked, 'What part of speech is *watch*?' or 'What part of speech is *iron*?' the right answer is, 'I don't know. But if you put the word into a sentence, then I can give you the answer.'

Now why is this? It's because **you tell what part of speech a word is by the work it is doing**. So you must see (or hear) the word at work in a sentence.

For example, take *watch* in the sentence,
    My father gave me a new *watch* for my birthday.
In that sentence *watch* is the name of something, and so it is a **noun**.

Now look at this sentence,
    I am going to *watch* a football match.
Here, of course, *watch* expresses an action: it tells what I am going to *do*. So in this sentence *watch* is a **verb**.

5

Lesson One

What about this sentence?

No thieves can come to our house because we have a good *watch* dog.

What kind of dog? – a *watch* dog. As you know, words that tell 'what kind' are adjectives. So here, *watch* is an **adjective** qualifying the noun *dog*.

Or take the word *spring* in these three sentences:

1 The *spring* of my watch is broken.
2 The dog tried to *spring* over the gate.
3 I love *spring* flowers.

In 1 it is the name of something – a **noun**.
In 2 it expresses an action – a **verb**.
In 3 it tells what kind of flowers – an **adjective**.

So remember:
You tell what part of speech a word is by the work it does.

Exercises

A What part of speech are the words in *italics*?

Example: *Turn* to the right at the *corner*.
Answer: Turn – verb; corner – noun

1 Use a big *hammer* for those *nails*.
2 *Hammer* the *nails* in well.
3 *Nail* the picture on the wall.
4 I can *answer* that question.
5 Give me the *answer* to the question.
6 We are going to *stay* in Athens.
7 Our *stay* there will be for only a week.

8 We *drink* tea from tea-cups.
9 Will you come and have a *drink*?
10 My father likes to *smoke* a pipe.
11 The *smoke* is going up the chimney.

B Give the part of speech of the words in *italics*.

1 *Bath* the baby in the small *bath*, and dry him with the *bath* towel.
2 John's mother is using an electric *iron* to *iron* John's shirt.
3 That *iron* gate is made of *iron* that came from England.
4 These *plants* need *water*. You must *water* them every day in dry weather.
5 I am going to *plant* some *water*-lilies in my pond.
6 I want you to *colour* these pictures any *colour* you like.

C Use the following words in sentences (a) as **nouns** and (b) as **verbs**.

Example: film
Answer: (a) Have you seen the new *film* at the Odeon?
          (b) They *filmed* some of the scenes in Rome.

1 walk   3 work   5 use   7 box
2 fire   4 wish   6 wave   8 rain

D Here is a short story.

Newspaper headlines

My Harlow newspaper had a big headline: GERMAN WORKS FOR HARLOW.

There was a picture of a German businessman, and I read these words under the picture: *Mr Schwarz in Harlow yesterday*.

'That's the man,' I thought.
'That's the German, but what
does he *do* for Harlow?'
I began to read the article.

GERMAN WORKS FOR HARLOW

Car assembly works plan

Final arrangements have been made for the German firm of
Schwarz to assemble their Lakeland and Riverside cars in
Harlow. The company plans to build the works on sixty
acres of land close to Harlow. When assembly starts, several hundred Harlow people will work there. Mr Schwarz,
the managing director, expects to open the factory in March
next year.

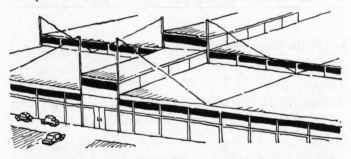

12 words are underlined in the headlines and the article.
Say what **part of speech** each word is in the sentence you
find it in. We have done the first two words for you as an
example.

Examples: GERMAN – adjective
WORKS   – noun

Lesson Two

Nouns

Revision (Book 1, Lessons 2–5). A **noun** is the **name** of anything. Nouns that are the names for all people or things or places of the same kind are **common nouns**. The special names of people, places or things are **proper nouns. Proper nouns** all begin with a capital letter.

Nouns can be **singular** or **plural.**

The **possessive** of **singular nouns** is formed by putting *'s* after the noun that stands for the possessor.

The **possessive** of **plural nouns** is formed by putting an apostrophe after the noun if the plural ends in *s* (*boys' shoes*) or by putting *'s* after the noun if the plural does not end in *s* (*children's shoes*).

The **possessive** form is not generally used for nouns that name things, only for people (and for most animals).

Abstract nouns

There are some other kinds of nouns. Look at these sentences:

The car went at a speed of 90 miles an hour.

Thank you for your great kindness.

Lloyd has toothache.

He bore the pain with great courage.

Health is better than wealth.

The words *speed, kindness, toothache, pain, courage, health, wealth* are all **nouns.** Each of them is the name of something. But they are not quite like the other nouns that you have met so far. They don't really name things. They name qualities or ideas. They don't name things you can touch or see. You can see and touch the tooth, but you can't see the 'ache'. *Toothache* is an **abstract noun**.

The nouns *kindness, speed, health,* etc. don't name material things; they name abstract things. We call nouns like this **abstract nouns**.

Collective nouns

There are some **nouns** that are the names not of just one person or thing, but of a whole collection of people or things, considered as one.

For example, in the school's hockey team there are eleven players but we think of it as a single team, that is, as one thing. We call it a *team*. In this case, *team* is a **collective noun**.

Nouns that stand for a number of things considered as one are called **collective nouns**. Collective nouns generally (but not always) take a singular verb.

The crowd *was* one of the largest I have ever seen.

A flock of sheep *is* coming down the hill.

The class *has* an English lesson every day.

Exercises

A Pick out the **abstract nouns** in these sentences.

Example: Some British people don't like the heat.
Answer: heat

1 The soldiers fought with great courage.
2 He has always had very good health.
3 The flight of the birds is very beautiful.
4 I made this table without any help.
5 That flower is a pretty colour.
6 He was filled with admiration for my skill in rowing the boat.
7 The explorer was suffering from hunger and thirst but was full of hope of success.
8 There is wisdom in the old man's advice.
9 I want you to get the measurements of this room. Write down its length, breadth, and height.

10 We all admire beauty not ugliness; strength not
    weakness; bravery not cowardice; kindness not cruelty;
    generosity not meanness.

B Pick out the **collective nouns** in these sentences.

Example: The team was chosen by a committee.
Answer: team, committee

1 The man was driving a herd of cattle.
2 That ship has a crew of a hundred men.
3 He has a whole library of books.
4 A swarm of bees flew out of the hive.
5 The audience listened in breathless silence to the singer.
6 The regiment of soldiers marched into battle.
7 A pack of wolves chased the sledge.
8 The fishermen saw a big shoal of fish.
9 The police were trying to control the mob.
10 Men are wanted for the army, the navy and the air force.

C Pick out the **nouns** in the following story and arrange them
in columns under these headings.

Common	Proper	Abstract	Collective
man morning	Pat	cold hunger	family

We have done the first two sentences as an example.

Wit can gain a breakfast

Pat was a poor man with a large family. One morning, cold
and hunger made him wake up early. He decided to go
shooting in a wood near his cottage.

The wood belonged to Lord Northwood, a rich gentle-
man, and Pat had no right to go there. But there were
families of rabbits in the wood, and Pat determined to take

the risk. Suddenly he saw the owner, with a group of friends, coming towards him through the wood. There was a look of anger on Lord Northwood's face as he caught sight of the gun in Pat's hands. Pat's heart sank with fear, but he saw there was no hope of escape. So he walked boldly towards the company and said to Lord Northwood, 'Good morning, sir. What has brought you out so early this morning?'

Lord Northwood was rather surprised but he said, 'My friends and I are taking a little exercise to get an appetite for our breakfast.' Then, looking at Pat with suspicion, he said, 'But why are *you* out so early in the morning?'

'Well, sir,' said Pat, 'I just came out to try to get a breakfast for my appetite.'

The whole crowd burst into laughter at Pat's ready wit, and with a smile Lord Northwood walked on, leaving Pat to try his luck with the rabbits.

Lesson Three

Plurals of nouns

Revision (Book 1, Lessons 2 and 3). **Singular nouns** generally make their **plurals** by adding *s*.
Some (ending in a 'hissing sound' or in *-o*) add *-es*.
Some (ending in *-f* or *-fe*) change to *-ves*.
Some (ending in *-y*) change to *-ies*.

In Book 1, you saw the principal methods of forming the plural. Here are some more points about **plural nouns**.

1 A few **nouns** have the same form for **singular** and **plural**.
Two common ones are *sheep* and *deer*.

    There is a *sheep* in that field. (singular)
    There are some *sheep* in that field. (plural)
    I saw a *deer* in the woods. (singular)
    I saw two *deer* in the woods. (plural)

Usually *fish* has the same form in the **singular** as in the **plural**.

    How many *fish* have you caught today? (plural)
    We have only caught one *fish* today. (singular)

2 Some **nouns** have no plural: *information, advice, furniture, news*. So we say,

    I bought three pieces of furniture (*never* three furnitures).
    He gave me two good bits of advice (not two advices).
    The news *is* good (*never* the news *are* good).
News looks like a plural word, but it isn't.

Pence is the usual **plural** for *penny*.
   This rubber cost ten *pence*.
Some people *say p* instead of *pence*.
   'I paid ten p for it.'
But you should write *pence*.

3 Some **nouns** have no singular: *scissors, trousers, clothes, riches*.
   These scissors *are* not sharp. (or *This* pair of scissors *is* not sharp.)
   Tommy's trousers *were* torn as he was climbing the tree.
   Her clothes *are* always very smart.
   Riches *do* not always bring happiness.

4 There are some **nouns** that are made up of two nouns: *schoolroom, girlfriend, boyfriend, bookcase, workman*.
In the plural, only the second part changes.

Singular	Plural
classroom	classrooms
girlfriend	girlfriends
boyfriend	boyfriends
bookcase	bookcases
workman	workmen

Exercises

A Make the following sentences **plural**.

Example: The fisherman caught a fish in his net.
Answer: The fishermen caught (some) fish in their nets.

1 There is a deer on the hillside.
2 This sheep is white, but that sheep is black.
3 The bookcase is made of oak.

4 I am going to pay the workman.
5 My grandfather is coming to visit me.
6 He is a schoolboy but he isn't at school today.
7 A sheep is eating a cabbage in my garden.
8 She has invited her boyfriend to the party.
9 That newspaper used to cost a penny. (Use *two* in your answer).

B Put the missing verbs (*is, are, was, were*) in the following sentences. Write **singular** or **plural** after each sentence.

Example: The boy's trousers ____ torn.
Answer: The boy's trousers were torn. (plural)

1 There ____ some bad news in the paper this morning.
2 His clothes ____ made by a good tailor.
3 That furniture ____ very dear.
4 The advice that he gave me ____ good.
5 The people in that room ____ waiting for me.
6 My scissors ____ not very sharp.
7 This information ____ just what I want.
8 All the fish in the pond ____ gold and red.

Determiners:
possessive adjectives 1

In all those sentences there are words that show who those various cats belong to: *my* cat, *your* cat, *his* cat, and so on.

These words (all qualifying the noun *cat*) are **adjectives**. Because they show possession, we call them **possessive adjectives**. Let's collect them and arrange them like this:

Determiners: possessive adjectives		
	Singular	*Plural*
1st person	my	our
2nd person	your	your
3rd person	his, her, its	their

When we use a **possessive adjective** with a **noun,** the noun does not have any other **determiner** (like *a, an, the, this, some*).

Exercises

A In the blank spaces in the following, write first the **possessive adjective** and then the **personal pronoun (objective)**. The first one is done for you.

1 I have a book. This is _my_ book. I have brought it with _me._

2 You have a book. This is ____ book. You have brought it with ____.

3 He has a book. This is ____ book. He has brought it with ____.

4 She has a book. This is ____ book. She has brought it with ____.

5 It (the dog) has a bone. This is ____ bone. It has brought it with ____.

6 We have a book. This is ____ book. We have brought it with ____.

7 They have a book.　　　This is ___ book. They have
　　　　　　　　　　　　brought it with ____.

B Write these sentences with **possessive adjectives** instead
of the words in *italics*.

Example: This is *the* key *that belongs to me*.
Answer: This is *my* key.

1 The mother told *the mother's* little girl a story.
2 Tom rode *Tom's* bicycle to school.
3 The little bird built *the little bird's* nest in the tree.
4 Susan gave a present to *Susan's* friend.
5 The teacher told Richard to bring *Richard's* book to the
　desk.
6 I have lost *the* penknife *that belongs to me*.
7 Mr and Mrs Robinson have just gone into *Mr and Mrs
　Robinson's* house.
8 We have sold *the* car *that belonged to us*.
9 The dog is in *the* basket *that is the dog's*.
10 I want *the* book *that belongs to me*, not *the* book *that
　belongs to you*.

Lesson Five

Determiners: possessive adjectives 2

You have learned what the **possessive adjectives** are. Now we must notice three points about the way they behave.

1 The **singular** forms *my, your, his, her, its* are used if the **possessor** is singular. It doesn't matter whether the thing that is possessed is singular or plural.

A few examples will make the matter quite clear. Take the possessive adjective *my*, which is singular, and put a **singular** noun with it.

My sister is in the house.

Now we will use a **plural** noun with it.

My sisters are in the garden.

In some languages, French or German, for example, when the noun is plural, the possessive adjective is plural too. In English it isn't. Here are some more examples.

My { pocket is full of apples.
   { pockets are full of apples.

His { book is on the table.
    { books are on the table.

Her { friend is coming to tea.
    { friends are coming to tea.

Your { window is broken.
     { windows are broken.

2 The **plural** forms *our, your, their* are used if the **possessor** is plural. It doesn't matter whether the thing possessed is singular or plural.

Our cat (singular) is in the basket.
Our cats (plural) are in their basket.

I have just been talking to your brother (singular).
I have just been talking to your brothers (plural).

They are walking with their son (singular).

They are walking with their sons (plural).

3 *His* is **masculine**, *her* is **feminine**. *My, your, our, their* are
used for **masculine** or **feminine**. *Its* is used for **neutral gender
singular**, *their* is used for **neutral gender plural**.

If the **possessor** is male, the **possessive adjective** is **masculine**.
If the **possessor** is female, the **possessive adjective** is **feminine**.
It doesn't matter which gender the thing possessed is. For
example:

    She is carrying *her* cat.
    He is carrying *his* cat.
    The tree is losing *its* leaves.

21

Mary is walking with *her* mother.

Tom is walking with *his* mother.

Francine is walking with *her* father.

The mother is walking with *her* son.

The father is walking with *his* daughter.

Susan is carrying *her* brother.

John is carrying *his* sister.

And here you can see all these uses of the **possessive adjectives**.

I have a name; *my* name is Tom.
You have a name; *your* name is Pauline.
She has a name; *her* name is Susan.
It has a name; *its* name is Jumbo the Elephant.
We have a name; *our* name is Brown.
You have a name; *your* name is Green.
They have a name; *their* name is Robinson.

Exercises

A Make sentences of your own, using *my, your, his, her, its, our, their*.

B Here is a short story. Rewrite it with **possessive adjectives** in the blank spaces and instead of the words in *italics*.

Dr Swift and the boy

More than two hundred years ago, the writer Jonathan Swift lived near a rich old lady. The lady sometimes sent a boy with a present for Swift. Swift took *the lady's* presents gladly, but he never gave the boy anything for ____ trouble. One day Swift was busy with ____ writing, when the boy rushed into *Swift's* room, knocked some books out of *the books'* place, threw ____ parcel on the desk and said, '____ mistress has sent you two of ____ rabbits.'

Swift turned round and said, 'That is not the way to deliver ____ parcel. Now, you sit in ____ chair and watch ____ way of doing it.'

The boy sat down. Swift went out, knocked on *Swift's* door and waited. The boy said, 'Come in.' Swift entered, walked to ____ desk and said, 'If you please, sir, ____ mistress sends ____ kind regards and hopes you will accept these rabbits which ____ son shot this morning in ____ fields.'

The boy answered, 'Thank you, ____ boy. Give ____ mistress and ____ son *Dr Swift's* thanks for ____ kindness and here is sixpence for yourself.'

Swift laughed, and after that, he never forgot to give the boy ____ tip.

Comparison of adjectives 1

Mr Bingo is a *strong* man. Mr Jingo is *stronger*. Mr Stingo is the *strongest* man of the three.

Mr Bingo, Mr Jingo and Mr Stingo are all strong in different **degrees**, and we show that by three different forms of the **adjective**: strong, strong*er*, *the* strong*est*.

In grammar, these three forms are called the **positive** degree, the **comparative** degree, and the **superlative** degree.

A great many short adjectives form their comparative degree by adding -*er*, and their superlative by adding -*est* to the positive.

Positive	Comparative	Superlative
tall	taller	the tallest
short	shorter	the shortest
quick	quicker	the quickest
old	older	the oldest

Sometimes the last letter of the **positive** is doubled:

Positive	Comparative	Superlative
hot	hotter	the hottest
fat	fatter	the fattest
big	bigger	the biggest
thin	thinner	the thinnest

If the **positive** ends in -*e* we only add -*r* and -*st*:

Positive	Comparative	Superlative
large	larger	the largest
fine	finer	the finest

Adjectives that end in -*y* usually change this to -*ier* in the **comparative** and -*iest* in the **superlative**:

Positive	Comparative	Superlative
pretty	prettier	the prettiest
happy	happier	the happiest
heavy	heavier	the heaviest

Exercises

A What are the three **degrees** of comparison?

B Give the **comparative** and the **superlative** of the following adjectives:

1 high	4 bright	7 mad	10 happy
2 lazy	5 new	8 thin	11 large
3 long	6 hot	9 red	12 pretty

Comparison of adjectives 2

You have just seen one way in which **adjectives** form their **comparative** and **superlative**: they add *-er* and *-est* to the **positive**.

Comparison of long adjectives

Some adjectives form their **comparative** and **superlative** by using *more* and *most*.

This is an exciting book.

This is a *more* exciting book.

This is *the most* exciting book of all.

The **adjectives** that do this are usually rather long words. All **adjectives** of three or more syllables, e.g. ex-cit-ing, in-terest-ing, un-for-tu-nate, are compared like this.

Here are some more examples:

Positive	Comparative	Superlative
important	more important	the most important
dangerous	more dangerous	the most dangerous
valuable	more valuable	the most valuable
wonderful	more wonderful	the most wonderful
convenient	more convenient	the most convenient

Irregular comparison

Unfortunately, 'rules' in English grammar always have 'exceptions', some disobedient words that won't obey the rules. Well, there are some 'exceptions' to these rules for **comparison of adjectives**. Take *good* for example. We can't say ~~gooder~~ and ~~goodest~~. And we can't say ~~badder~~ and ~~baddest~~. We'll just gather these 'disobedient' words together.

Irregular comparatives and superlatives		
Positive	*Comparative*	*Superlative*
good	better	the best
bad	worse	the worst
far	farther	the farthest
	further	the furthest

Comparing one thing with another

Look at these three ways of comparing one thing (or person) with another.

1 With the **positive** degree we use *as* before the **adjective** and *as* after it.

This stick is *as* long *as* that one.

John is not *as* fat *as* his father.

27

2 With the **comparative** we use ... *than* after the **adjective**.
  That stick is *longer than* this one.
  This horse is *better than* that one.
  That's a *more comfortable* chair *than* this chair.

3 After the superlative we often use *of*.
  This is *the best of* the three knives.
But we may use a phrase that begins *in, on* etc.
  That girl is *the youngest in* the class.
  He's *the biggest* boy *on* the field.

Exercises

A Give the **comparative** and the **superlative** of the
following **adjectives**.

1 wide	4 good	7 useful	10 far
2 dangerous	5 fortunate	8 nice	11 greedy
3 difficult	6 bad	9 beautiful	12 magnificent

B Fill in the missing words.

1 Tom is older ____ Richard.
2 Fred is not ____ old ____ Tom.
3 Tom is ____ oldest ____ the three.
4 This book is better ____ that.
5 This book is not ____ good ____ that.
6 This book is ____ best ____ the three.
7 That exercise is more difficult ____ this one.

8 The weather is worse today ____ it was yesterday.
9 It was not ____ bad yesterday ____ it is today.
10 Today's weather is ____ worst ____ the week.

C Write out these sentences. Put the **adjectives** that are in brackets into their correct form. (Some are already in the correct form. Leave them as they are.)

1 Tom is (old) than Richard.
2 John is the (clever) boy in the class.
3 The weather is (fine) today than it was yesterday.
4 Cairo is the (big) city in Egypt.
5 This sentence is (difficult) than the first one.
6 My bicycle is as (good) as yours.
7 My bicycle is (good) than yours.
8 My bicycle is the (good) of the three.
9 Your bicycle is (old) than mine.
10 My cold is (bad) today than it was yesterday.
11 This mountain is the (high) in Europe.
12 This piece of homework is as (bad) as your last one.
13 This piece of homework is (bad) than your last one.
14 This piece of homework is the (bad) of all your exercises.
15 Richard is not as (tall) as Tom.
16 Tom is (tall) than Richard.
17 Tom is the (tall) boy in the class.
18 Tokyo is (far) from London than Rome is.
19 Mr Chung is (rich) than Mr Huang, but I don't think he is (happy) than Mr Huang.
20 Their hens are (good) than ours. They are the (good) in the country.

D Answer the following questions.

1 Tom is taller than Richard, and Richard is taller than Fred. Which of the boys is the tallest? Which is the shortest?

2 It is hotter in Athens than it is in London. It is not as hot in Oslo as it is in London. Which of the three cities is the hottest? Which is the coldest?

3 Richard got worse marks than Fred in the examination. John got worse marks than Richard. Which boy got the best marks? Which boy got the worst?

4 A train goes faster than a ship but not as fast as an aeroplane. Which is the fastest? Which is the slowest?

Lesson Eight

Determiners:
the articles *a, an, the*

We mentioned the **determiners** on page 18. The **determiners** are a small number of words that we use with **nouns**. Here are most of the **determiners**:

Definite article: *the*
Indefinite article: *a, an.*
Demonstrative adjectives: *this, that, these, those* (Book 1, Lesson 8)
Possessive adjectives: *my, your, his, her, its, our, your, their* (Book 2, Lesson 4)
every, each, either
some

Determiners are often used with **adjectives**:
  I've lost *a big red* book.
  This is *your big red* book, isn't it?
  No. *That red* book isn't as big as my book.

But **determiners** are never used with other **determiners**. You never say ~~a this book~~ or ~~the my book~~ or ~~my the book~~ or ~~each these books~~.

The definite article

We call *a, an* and *the* **articles**. *The* is the **definite article**. We use *the* with **nouns** that name:

31

1 people or things when the hearer or reader knows who or
what we mean – when the meaning is **definite**.

> I have been talking to *the head teacher*. (We know which
> head teacher.)
> He is going to *the post office*. (We know which post
> office.)

2 a person or thing that is the only one.

> We get light from *the sun* and *the moon*.
> *The River Thames* flows through London.

Pronounce *the* with an *ee* sound before a vowel sound: *the
Alps, the end, the index, the hour* (we don't sound the *h*).

The indefinite article

We call *a, an* the **indefinite article**. We use *a* or *an* with
common nouns when we mention somebody or something for
the first time.

> There's *a good film* at the Odeon.
> *A man* ran towards us with *a knife*.

If we mention the person or thing again, we know which one,
so we use *the*.

> There's *a good film* at the Odeon. *The film* is about
> cowboys.
> *A man* ran towards us with *a knife*. *The knife* was red with
> blood, and *the man* was shouting.

RICHARD: What's the difference between *a* and *an*?
TEACHER: Well, here are some examples:

a boy	*an* apple
a house	*an* ear
a big egg	*an* Indian song
a dog	*an* orange

Now can you tell me the answer?

RICHARD: Oh yes, I see it. If the next word begins with a
consonant sound, you use *a*, but if it begins with a vowel

sound, you use *an*.

TEACHER: That's right. Notice also that with words like *hour, honour, honest,* we use *an* because the *h* is not sounded. So we say *an honest man, an hour ago*, etc.

Originally *a (an)* meant one. 'Tom has *an* apple' means 'Tom has *one* apple'. And notice that the beginning of the next word makes us choose *a* or *an*. So we say

There was *a car* outside the door.

There was *a new car* outside the door.

There was *an old car* outside the door.

We saw *an elephant*.

We saw *a young elephant*. (*Young* doesn't begin with a vowel sound.)

We saw *an old elephant*.

Can *a* or *an* go with any **common noun**, John?

JOHN: Oh, no; only if the noun is **singular**.

TEACHER: Of course! You can say *a book* but not ~~a books~~. You can say *a woman* but not ~~a women~~. The plural of *a book* is *books* or *some books*. Here are a few examples:

Singular	Plural
A horse is a useful animal.	Horses are useful animals.
An apple grows on a tree.	Apples grow on trees.
There is a book on the table.	There are books (*or* some books) on the table.

Exercises

A Put *a* or *an* before each of the following words:

1 cat	4 hour	7 horse
2 pen	5 telephone	8 ice-cream
3 eye	6 aeroplane	9 honour

When do you use *a* and when do you use *an*?

B Write *a* or *an* before these pairs of words – **adjective** and **noun**.

Examples: old man, tall man, big orange
Answers: an old man, a tall man, a big orange

1 long road	6 nice egg
2 ugly man	7 hard question
3 easy answer	8 old person
4 easy question	9 young animal
5 enormous box	10 Jamaican friend

C Mark the **determiners** in this story. There are 14 of them.

A girl received a very nice ring from her boyfriend. She wore the ring to the office the next day. Nobody noticed it. She moved her hand this way and that way, and still none of the other girls in the office noticed the ring. At last she said, 'It's a very hot day, isn't it? I must take off my ring.'

How many **indefinite articles** did you find?
How many times is the **definite article** used in the story?
What other **determiners** have you marked in the story?

Lesson Nine

Countable and uncountable nouns

TEACHER: Can you use *a* or *an* with any **singular noun**, Alan?

ALAN: I've been thinking about that. I thought of the nouns *bread* and *steam*. I wouldn't say *a* or *an* before those nouns. So I think the answer to your question is 'No'. But I'm not sure which nouns can have *a* and which nouns can't.

TEACHER: Well done, Alan. Listen to this carefully:

All common nouns can be divided into two classes: countable nouns and uncountable nouns.

Nouns like *apples, boys, bicycles, aeroplanes* are **countable** – that is to say, you can count the things they name. You can have three bicycles, ten boys, twenty aeroplanes, fifty apples.

But what about things like *water, air, bread, money, wool, smoke, glass, rain*? You don't say: ~~Count the waters coming out of this tap~~ or ~~How many airs are there in this room~~? or ~~Please count these moneys~~. You could, perhaps, count *drops* of water, *slices* of bread, *pieces* of money. The words (**nouns**) *drops, slices, pieces* are **countables**, but *water, bread, money* are **uncountables**. Do you think you see the difference?

ALAN: Oh yes, I think so.

RICHARD: You used the noun *glass* as an example of the **uncountables**. But can't I say, 'There are three *glasses* on the table'? So isn't *glass* in that sentence a **countable** noun?

TEACHER: Yes, Richard, it is. You see, a word in English often has more than one meaning. If, as in your sentence, *glass* means 'a thing we can drink out of', then it is a

countable noun. But if *glass* names the stuff that windows are made of, it is an **uncountable** noun. In the sentence, 'My house is built of stone,' the word *stone*, for the stuff my house is made of, is **uncountable**. But if I say, 'The boys threw *stones* through the window,' *stone* would be a **countable** noun. So the rule is:

You can use *a* (*an*) with a singular countable noun. You can't use *a* (*an*) with uncountable nouns.

You hardly ever use a **singular countable noun** without a **determiner**.

Glass is used for windows. (*Glass* is **uncountable**.)
I want *a glass* for my orange drink. (*Glass* is **countable** and it has the **determiner** *a*.)

Exercises

A Arrange the **nouns** in the box in two columns: **countable nouns** in column 1 and **uncountable nouns** in column 2. We have put the first two nouns in the correct columns for you.

> gold, machine, tree, silver, happiness, flower, flour, machinery, wool, spoon, milk, electricity, tea, steam, book, house, rain, cigarette, mud, wheel, cotton, teacher, education, butter, hat, shoe, leather, goodness, grass, pen, paper, corn.

1. Countable nouns	2. Uncountable nouns
machine	gold

B Copy out these sentences putting *a* or *an* where necessary. Remember that only **countable nouns** that are **singular** take *a* or *an*. Don't put anything before a plural countable noun or an uncountable noun.

1 That is ____ man.
2 These are ____ men.
3 ____ house can be built of ____ stone.
4 ____ cow is ____ animal.
5 ____ cows are ____ animals.
6 ____ cigarette is made of ____ tobacco and ____ paper.
7 ____ chair is made of ____ wood.
8 ____ chairs are made of ____ wood.
9 ____ man must have ____ air to live.
10 ____ hen can lay ____ egg.
11 ____ flower grows in ____ garden.
12 ____ flowers grow in ____ gardens.
13 We get ____ milk from ____ cow.
14 We get ____ milk from ____ cows.
15 ____ window is made of ____ glass.
16 ____ rain falls from the sky.
17 ____ shoe is made of ____ leather.
18 ____ shoes are made of ____ leather.
19 ____ grass grows in ____ English field.
20 ____ grass grows in ____ English fields.
21 ____ record-player plays ____ music.
22 You put ____ record on ____ record-player to get ____ music.
23 ____ flour is made from ____ wheat.
24 ____ loaf is made from ____ flour.
25 ____ loaves are made from ____ flour.

C Put these sentences into the **singular**.

Example: There are some birds in those trees. They are
    building nests.
Answer: There is a bird in that tree. It is building a nest.

1 Some books are on my desk.
2 Roses are flowers.
3 Dogs are animals.
4 Houses are buildings.
5 Chairs are pieces of furniture.
6 Nouns are the names of things.
7 Knives are made of steel.
8 Carpenters work with hammers and saws.
9 People light cigarettes with matches.
10 Dogs have tails.
11 Jackets are made of cloth.
12 Oaks are big trees.
13 Soldiers carry guns.
14 Horses are useful to farmers.
15 Bridges are often made of stone.

D Here is a little story.

The trapper and the weather

Two men were travelling in a very wild and lonely part of
America. For days they didn't see a house, only a few huts
made of wood, or tents made of skins. Then one day they
met an old man who trapped animals for their fur. They had
a conversation with him.

One of them asked him, 'Can you tell us what the
weather will be like in the next few days?'

'Oh yes,' he said. 'Rain is coming, and wind. Then there
will be snow for two days, but after that there will be bright
sunshine.'

'Isn't that wonderful?' said one man to his friend. 'These

old trappers know more of the secrets of Nature than we do with all our science.'

He turned to the old trapper. 'How do you know all that?' he asked.

'I heard it on the radio.'

Pick out six **uncountable nouns** in that story, and ten **countable nouns**.

Verbs: tense 1

Revision (Book 1, Lessons 9 to 12). **Verbs** are used to express an action or a state of being. There is always a **verb** in the **predicate** of a sentence. If the **subject** of a sentence is **singular**, the **verb** is **singular**; if the **subject** is **plural**, the **verb** is **plural**. Verbs that take **objects** are **transitive verbs**. Verbs that don't take **objects** are **intransitive verbs**.

TEACHER: What day *is* it today?
PUPIL: It *is* Tuesday today.
TEACHER: What day *was* it yesterday?
PUPIL: It *was* Monday yesterday.
TEACHER: What day *will* it *be* tomorrow?
PUPIL: It *will be* Wednesday tomorrow.

In those questions and answers we have been talking about three different times. The first question and its answer are about the **present** time: *today*. The second pair are about **past** time: *yesterday*. The third are about **future** time: *tomorrow*. Here are some other examples:

ELIZABETH: (A) This year I *am* in the 2nd Year English Class.

(B) Last year I *was* in the 1st Year English Class.

(C) Next year I *will* (I'*ll*) *be* in the 3rd Year English Class.

COLETTE: (A) I *have* a flower in my coat today.

(B) I *had* one in my coat yesterday.

(C) I *will* (I'*ll*) *have* another one tomorrow.

TEACHER: (A) This week the students *do* their lessons in Room 4.

(B) Last week they *did* them in Room 3.

(C) Next week they *will* (they'*ll*) *do* them in Room 5.

Sentences (A) are about **present** time: *this year*, *today*, *this week*.

Sentences (B) are about **past** time: *last year*, *yesterday*, *last week*.

Sentences (C) are about **future** time: *next year*, *tomorrow*, *next week*.

As you can see, the verbs have a different form to show these different times.

Present	Past	Future
am	was	will be
have	had	will have
do	did	will do

These different forms are called **tenses**.

The present tense is used for actions in present time.

The past tense is used for actions in past time.

The future tense is used for actions in future time.

WAS — PAST
IS — PRESENT
WILL BE — FUTURE

41

Here is the **simple present tense**, the **simple past tense** and the **future tense** of the verbs *be* and *have*.

Simple present tense	Simple past tense	Future tense
be		
I am he, she, it is we are you are they are	I was he, she, it was we were you were they were	I he, she, it we } will be/ you 'll be they
have		
I have he, she, it has we have you have they have	I he, she, it we } had you they	I he, she, it we } will have/ you 'll have they

You will hear *shall* after *I* or *we*, but there is no need to use it.

Exercises

A Copy out and complete these in the **present tense**.

I	am	a student.
He She John Mary }	——	————
We	are	————
You	——	a student.
You	——	students.
They Those boys }	——	————

B Copy out and complete these in the **past tense**.

I	had	a holiday in	_____ last year.
He My brother	_____	_____	_____
She My sister	_____	_____	_____
We My sister and I	_____	_____	_____ last month.
You	_____	_____	_____
They My brother and sister	_____	_____	_____

C Copy out and complete these in the **future tense**.

I	will be	here	tomorrow.
My brother	_____	_____	_____
My sister	_____	_____	_____
We	_____	in Paris	next month.
My father	_____	_____	_____

D Put these sentences into the **simple past tense**. Add one of the words or phrases in the box to show past time.

> yesterday, last week, until yesterday, two years ago, when I was younger, last month

1 I am in school.
2 He is a good swimmer.
3 The flowers are very beautiful.
4 Tom has five pence in his pocket.
5 The sun is very hot.
6 Mary has a new pen.
7 I am Richard's friend.
8 Velma has a new book.
9 The children are not ready for school.
10 We have plenty of time to get to school.

43

Lesson Eleven

Verbs: tense 2

Here is the verb *do*:

do		
Simple present tense	*Simple past tense*	*Future tense*
I do he she } does it we do you do they do	I did he she } did it we did you did they did	I will do/'ll do he she } will do/'ll do it we will do/'ll do you will do/'ll do they will do/'ll do

Here are some more sentences using the verbs *be*, *have*, *do* in the three tenses.

Present tense

MARY: Today *is* my birthday, so I *have* a holiday today. On my birthday I always *do* my work early in the morning, so I *am* free for the day. This year my birthday *is* on a Tuesday. I *have* a present for my birthday, here it *is* in my hand. I *am* eleven years old today.

Past tense

JANE: It *was* my birthday yesterday, so I *had* a holiday then. I *did* my work early in the morning, so I *was* free for the day. I *had* a present for my birthday. I *was* twelve years old yesterday.

Future tense

PAULINE: It *will be* my birthday tomorrow, so I'*ll have* a holiday then. I'*ll do* my work early in the morning, so I'*ll be* free for the day. My birthday *will be* on a Wednesday this year. I'*ll have* a party, and my mother and father *will give* me a birthday present. I'*ll be* thirteen years old tomorrow.

The tense of a verb shows the time (present, past, future) when the action happens, happened, or will happen.

Exercises

A Put the **verbs** in these sentences into the **simple present tense**. Change words, add them, or leave them out where necessary.

Example: We had breakfast at 7 o'clock yesterday.
Answer: We have breakfast at 7 o'clock every day.

1 He was a good footballer once.
2 We were in school yesterday.
3 The flowers were very beautiful last year.
4 The sun was very hot yesterday.
5 We were in the second class last year.
6 I did my lessons carefully.
7 Liz had tea at 5 o'clock.
8 The class did English three times a week last year.
9 I had a bad cold last week.
10 Harry was tired after the game of football.
11 The children's hands were very dirty.
12 You were very careless, weren't you?
13 Mary was here yesterday, wasn't she?

45

Lesson Eleven

B Put the **verbs** in the following sentences into the **future tense**. Change words where necessary, using, for example, *tomorrow*, *next year*, *in a few days' time*, *in five minutes*.

Example: We do our homework in the evening.
Answer: We will do our homework tomorrow.

1 I am twelve years old today.
2 You are in the second class this year.
3 I have plenty of time to finish the work.
4 They have a busy time today.
5 I do my work carefully.
6 Tom is a good swimmer.
7 It is a fine day today.
8 I am late for school.
9 The two boys are late for school.
10 The flowers are out in my garden.

Lesson Twelve

Present continuous tense

We have just learned that the **tense** of a verb shows the time of an action; it shows whether it happens in present time, past time, or future time.

But the tense of the verb can also show *whether the action is finished or not*. For example, look at these sentences:
I *am writing* on the blackboard.
You *are learning* grammar.
Tom *is reading* his book.
Mary *is studying* maths.
The flower *is dying*.
We *are singing* 'Ten Green Bottles'.
They *are fighting*.

All those actions are in the present time and they are all still continuing. The writing, learning, reading, singing, fighting are still going on; they are all still continuing. So this **verb** form is called the **present continuous tense**.

The present continuous tense expresses an action that is still going on now.

It is quite easy to make the **present continuous**. As you see, it has two parts. The first part is the **present tense** of the verb *be* (*am*, *is* or *are*). The second part is the form of the verb that ends in -*ing*: *learning*, *reading*, *singing*, etc. When you make the -*ing* form of a **verb**, notice these points of spelling:

1 Verbs that end in a silent -*e*, drop this -*e* when they add -*ing*: *dance*, *dancing*; *write*, *writing*; *save*, *saving*.
2 Some verbs double the last letter: *stop*, *stopping*; *get*, *getting*; *hit*, *hitting*.

47

3 Verbs ending in *-ie*, change this to *-y*: *lie*, *lying*; *die*, *dying*; *tie*, *tying*.

**The present continuous tense is made by using *am*, *is* or *are*
with the *-ing* form of the verb.**

Exercises

A Write down the *-ing* form of these **verbs**.

1 walk	5 dance	9 swim	13 reply
2 sing	6 write	10 save	14 die
3 talk	7 run	11 offer	15 lie
4 eat	8 dig	12 try	16 get

B Write out the **present continuous tense** for *I*, *she* and *we* of these **verbs**: *speak*, *take*, *cut*, *play*, *tie*.

Example: laugh
Answer: I am laughing. She is laughing. We are laughing.

C Change the **verbs** in these sentences from the **simple present tense** to the **present continuous tense**. Add a word or phrase from the box to each sentence. Leave out the words in brackets.

now, today, at this moment, at present

Example: My father (sometimes) uses a typewriter.
Answer: My father is using a typewriter at this moment.

1 I (often) write a letter.
2 Richard (always) walks to school.
3 We (usually) get up at six.
4 My mother (sometimes) works in the garden.
5 The old man lies down (after lunch).
6 He (often) stops the bus here.
7 We travel to Port of Spain (every day).
8 The gardener (sometimes) cuts down a tree.
9 John comes home (in the evening).
10 The shopkeeper (always) ties up the parcel.

Lesson Thirteen

Past continuous tense

Sometimes we want to speak of an action that was going on or continuing in the past time. In that case we use the **past tense** of the verb *be* with the *-ing* form of the **verb**.

Compare the **present continuous** and the **past continuous**.

 We *are looking* at this grammar book now. (present continuous)

 This time yesterday, we *were looking* at this grammar book. (past continuous)

Here are some other examples of the **past continuous tense**:

A year ago I *was working* in Barbados.

'I saw Richard at the station this morning.' – 'Yes, he *was waiting* for John, who *was coming* home from Oxford.'

Here is the **past continuous tense** of the verb *go*:

Singular		*Plural*	
1st person 2nd person 3rd person	I was going you were going he, she, it was going	1st person 2nd person 3rd person	we were going you were going they were going

The **past continuous** is very often used to show that an action was going on (or continuing) at a time when something else happened. An example will make that clear. Let's take an action that was still continuing:

'As I *was coming* to school this morning . . .'

Then something happened:

'. . . I *saw* a car run into a bus.'

Notice that the thing that suddenly happened is expressed by the **simple past tense** (*saw*). Here are some further examples:

Past Continuous (action going on)	*Simple past* (for new action)
The teacher *was giving* us a lesson	when a little dog *walked* into the room.
While we *were having* supper,	all the lights *went* out.
The fire *was* still *burning*	when I *passed* the house the next day.
While the man *was looking* in the shop window,	the thief *picked* his pocket.

Sometimes the sentences may be the other way round, with the verb in the **simple past tense** first, and the verb in the **past continuous tense** second:

Simple past	*Past continuous*
All the lights went out	while we were having supper.
When I passed the house next day,	the fire was still burning.
Harry did his homework	while the other boys were playing football.

Exercises

A Write out the **past continuous tense** of the verbs *do, rise, stop*.

B Put the verb in brackets into the **past continuous tense**.

1 John got off the train while it (go).
2 It (rain) when we went out.
3 I (play) the piano when he came into the room.
4 I came into the room when Lynette (play) the piano.
5 Joshua (work) all day yesterday.
6 She (live) in England when the war began.
7 He hurt his foot while he (climb) the tree.
8 The baby (eat) its dinner when I came home.
9 He (walk) home when the rain began.
10 The car hit a tree while it (travel) at 60 miles an hour.
11 He (write) a letter when I saw him.
12 The man fell down as he (run) for the bus.
13 We (sing) a song when Peter came into the room.
14 While the teacher (give) a lesson, a small dog walked into the room.
15 When the phone rang, I (work) in the garden.
16 My hat blew off while I (cross) the bridge.

Lesson Fourteen

Simple present tense and present continuous tense

Do you know when to use the **simple present tense** and when to use the **present continuous tense**? Compare these sentences.

(A) Mary plays the piano every evening.
(B) Mary is playing the piano now.
(A) You often write on the blackboard.
(B) You are writing on the blackboard now.

What is the difference between sentences (A) and sentences (B)?

The **present continuous tense** truly expresses an action in the present time, an action that is happening *now*. 'Mary is playing the piano' and 'I am writing on the blackboard' mean that these actions are going on at this very moment. They haven't ended when I say (or write) those sentences.

The **simple present tense** is generally used for an action that is done regularly, for an action that happens, perhaps, every day. So you often find words like *usually, generally, every day, sometimes, always* with it.

I am dancing now.
(present continuous)

I dance every day.
(simple present)

53

Now here is a short composition that Mark Brown wrote. It will show you the use of the **simple present tense**.

My daily programme – by Mark Brown

I *wake up* every day about seven o'clock. I *get* out of bed and *go* and *wake* Jeremy and Richard. I sometimes *drip* some water on them to wake them. Then they *get* up and *chase* me to the bathroom. We *wash*, and we *brush* our teeth and then we *go* back to the bedroom to dress. Mother usually *calls* upstairs, 'Come on, boys, breakfast is ready.' So we *hurry* downstairs. We *say*, 'Good morning, mother,' 'Good morning, father,' and *sit* down to breakfast. Father *goes* to the office at half-past eight, but before he *goes*, he usually *sits* and *reads* his paper. We *have* our breakfast and *ask* if we can leave the table. Then we *go* and *get* our books and school things. We *say* good-bye to mother, *take* out our bicycles and *cycle* to school.

As you see, all those verbs are in the **simple present tense** because Mark is telling you his daily habits. He is telling you what he does every day, not what he is doing at that moment.

The simple present tense is used for a repeated or habitual action.

The present continuous tense is used for an action that is still continuing now.

There are one or two small but rather important points that you should notice. In the **simple present tense** the **3rd person singular** ends in-*s*. (There are some exceptions, which you will meet in the next lesson.)

1st person singular	*3rd person singular*
I sit	he sits
I get	he gets
I read	he reads

Sometimes the 3rd person singular ends in *-es*.

I wash	he wash*es*
I go	he go*es*

Sometimes it changes from *-y* to *-ies*

I try	he tr*ies*
I cry	he cr*ies*

Exercises

A Here is the **simple present tense** of *eat*:

I eat	we eat
he, she, it eats	you eat
	they eat

Now write out the **simple present tense** of the verbs *get, sit, catch, smash, go, do*.

B Change the following from **1st person singular** to **3rd person singular.** Use the new subject given in brackets.

Example: I watch my school hockey team. (My brother)
Answer: My brother watches his school hockey team.

1 I like chocolate. (My sister)
2 I write the exercise. (He)
3 I know the answer. (She)
4 I try to do my work well. (Mary)
5 I wash my face and neck. (John)
6 I eat my breakfast. (My father)
7 I brush my teeth. (He)
8 I say good morning to my mother. (That boy)
9 I go to school on my bicycle. (This girl)

55

10 I do my work carefully. (A good lady teacher)
11 I can speak English. (He)
12 I will help you. (She)
13 I may come here tomorrow. (The cat)
14 I must finish my work. (My daughter)
15 I ought to be more careful. (Tom)

C In the following sentences the **verbs** have been left out.
Some of the verbs ought to be in the **present simple tense**,
others in the **present continuous tense**. Rewrite the sentences
putting in the verbs. (The verb to use is in brackets.)

Example: (cut) It's Saturday, and my brother ____ wood for
the fire. He always ____ wood on Saturdays.
Answer: It's Saturday, and my brother *is cutting* wood for
the fire. He always *cuts* wood on Saturdays.

1 (play) Elizabeth always ____ the piano well. She ____ it
now.
2 (drive) My mother ____ to her office every day. She ____
there now.
3 (rain) It ____ today. It usually ____ in winter.
4 (speak) He generally ____ Chinese, but he ____ English
today.
5 (make) Father ____ toast in the kitchen just now. He
usually ____ toast for breakfast.
6 (set) The sun always ____ in the west. It ____ now, and it
will soon be dark.
7 (dig) My sister always ____ the garden. She ____ it now.
8 (ring) The telephone ____ again. It sometimes ____
twenty times a day.
9 (do) John ____ his homework now. He usually ____ it in
the evening.
10 (go) Richard ____ to school every day.
11 (do) Careless students never ____ their work well.

12 (write) 'What is the teacher doing?' – 'He ____ on the blackboard.'
13 (live) That fat man ____ next door to us.
14 (go) He ____ just ____ in at the front door.
15 (strike) Listen, the clock ____. Count the strokes.
16 (go, give) Whenever we ____ to my aunt's house, she always ____ us a good tea.

D *Revision exercise on verbs.* Here is a story. Some of the verbs should be in the **simple present tense**, some in the **simple past tense**, some in the **past continuous** and some in the **future**. Rewrite the story with the verbs in the right forms.

The rich lady and the poor beggar

A wealthy lady (live) in a big hotel beside New York's Central Park. One day as she (look) out of the window, she (see) a very poor man dressed in rags. He (sit) on a wooden seat and he (look) up at the windows of the hotel. She (look) the next day and the next, and the next, and every day he (look) up at the windows of the hotel. At last one day while she (drive) in her car, she (stop) by the seat where the man (sit). She (get) out and (speak) to him and (ask) him why he (look) at the hotel windows.

'Lady,' he (say), 'I (sit) on this seat every day and I (sleep) on this seat every night, and all the time I (think) that some day I (sleep) in that hotel.'

The lady said, 'I (make) your dream come true. Tonight you (sleep) in the best room in the hotel.'

The next morning as she (sit) at breakfast she (see) the man and (call) him to come to her table. She (say), 'How did you sleep?'

'Lady,' he (say), 'my seat in the park was better.'

'Surely not,' (say) the lady.

'Yes,' he (say). 'You see, I (sleep) on the seat every night; but every night I (dream) I (be) in a soft warm bed in the hotel. But all last night while I (sleep), I dreamt that I was back on the cold hard seat. So I (go) back to my seat in the park tonight.'

Lesson Fifteen

Negative of verbs: 'method A' – the 'peculiars' 1

There are two main ways for **verbs** to form their **negatives**. Let's call them 'method A' and 'method B'.

There are only a few verbs that use 'method A', but they are verbs that are used very often. They are a strange little group. They don't behave like other verbs in a number of ways, so let's call them the 'peculiars'. Here are some of them:

be (am, is, are, was, were)	may
have (has, had)	might
can (could)	must
will (would)	ought to
shall (should)	

Others, which we will consider later, are *need*, *used to*, *do* (*does*, *did*) and *dare*.

The 'peculiars' form their negative simply by adding *not*.

And they are the only verbs out of the thousands of English verbs that make their **negative** in that way (the way we have called 'method A'). Here are some examples:

Affirmative	*Negative*
He is English.	He is *not* English.
She can speak English.	She can*not* speak English.
We will have a lesson tomorrow.	We will *not* have a lesson tomorrow.
You may have another cake.	You may *not* have another cake.
You must write in your book.	You must *not* write on the wall.
Tom ought to do his own work.	He ought *not* to ask Lloyd to do it for him.

Contracted forms

These negatives are often shortened, especially in conversation. Here are the contracted (shortened) forms:

Negative	*Contracted form*	*Negative*	*Contracted form*
is not	isn't	cannot	can't
are not	aren't	will not	won't
have not	haven't	must not	mustn't
has not	hasn't	ought not	oughtn't

Notice that the apostrophe (') takes the place of the *o* of *not*.

60

Exercises

A Write down the contracted forms of:

1 is not   3 are not   5 have not   7 will not
2 ought not   4 must not   6 has not   8 cannot

B Make the following sentences **negative**.

1 She is a teacher.
2 I am Greek.
3 You are my pupils.
4 We are your pupils.
5 Richard can swim very well.
6 I will go to see him tomorrow.
7 You ought to write your exercise in this book.
8 I will do what you ask me.
9 You must go now.
10 Have you any money? (Use the contracted form.)

Negative of verbs: 'method A' – the 'peculiars' 2

Here is the simple past tense of some of the 'peculiars':

Present tense	Past tense	Present tense	Past tense
am/is are	was were	have/has can	had could

Here are some examples:

He was in Tokyo yesterday.
She had a bicycle last year.

The other 'peculiars' do not have a past tense, but some of them can sometimes be used to express the meaning of others in the past. Here they are:

'Peculiar'	Past meaning sometimes expressed by
shall will may	should would might

Here are some examples:

I'll go now.
I wouldn't go before.
'We'll come to the party.'
They said they would come to the party.

The **negative** of these forms of the 'peculiars' is often shortened. Here are the contracted or short forms:

Negative	Short form	Negative	Short form
was not	wasn't	should not	shouldn't
had not	hadn't	would not	wouldn't
could not	couldn't	might not	mightn't
were not	weren't		

Some people think that the contracted forms can only be used in conversation. But nowadays you needn't be afraid to write them. Indeed, I advise you to use contracted forms in **negative questions**, even in serious writing.

Isn't English a useful world language?

Couldn't the Government help the poorer countries?

Here are some examples of the 'peculiars' in **affirmative** and **negative statements**:

Affirmative	*Negative*
He *was* here yesterday.	He *was not* (*wasn't*) here yesterday.
John *could* swim when he was six.	John *could not* (*couldn't*) swim when he was six.
He said that he *might* come.	He said that he *might not* (*mightn't*) come.
She said that she *would* help us.	She said that she *would not* (*wouldn't*) help us.

Exercises

A Write down the contracted (shortened) forms of:

1 was not   3 might not   5 had not
2 would not   4 should not   6 could not

B Make the following sentences **negative**.

1 Sidney was at our house last night.
2 John could swim when he was three years old.

3 Your friends were at the party last night.
4 He would go there if the weather was fine.
5 If the sky was clear, you could see the stars.

C In the second part of the sentence, use the **past** form
negative of the 'peculiar' that is in the first part.

Example: She's an old woman now, but she ____ old in 1950.
Answer: She's an old woman now, but she *wasn't* old in 1950.

1 There are two houses here now, but there ____ any houses
   here a year ago.
2 He has heard the news now, but he ____ heard it an hour
   ago.
3 There are a lot of computers in the world now, but there
   ____ a lot in 1960.
4 I've seen Paris now, but I ____ ever seen it before.
5 There's a cat in the garden this afternoon, but there ____
   one there this morning.

D In the second part of the sentence, use the same **verb** as in
the first part, but change the 'peculiar'.

Example: I can swim now, but I ____ when I was younger.
Answer: I can swim now, but I *couldn't swim* when I was
          younger.

1 He'll take us to the cinema next week, but he ____ us last
   week.
2 She can read his writing now, but she ____ it last year.
3 My friends will come with me this year but they ____ with
   me in 1984.
4 My grandfather could hear well a few years ago, but he
   ____ well now.
5 He wouldn't believe the story at first, but perhaps he ____
   it now.

Lesson Seventeen

Negative of verbs: present continuous and past continuous

You remember, of course, that the **present continuous tense** and the **past continuous tense** are formed by using parts of the verb *be* with the *-ing* form of the verb. So they form their **negative**, as the 'peculiars' do, simply by adding *not*.

Present continuous

Affirmative
I am writing on the blackboard.
You are learning English.

Negative
I *am not writing* (I'*m not writing*) on the blackboard.
You *are not* (*aren't*) *learning* English.

Ali is reading his history book.	Ali *is not* (*isn't*) *reading* his history book.
We are living in the twentieth century.	We *are not* (*aren't*) living in the eighteenth century.

Past continuous

Affirmative	*Negative*
He was working when I saw him.	He *was not* (*wasn't*) *working* when I saw him.
When I looked at the baby, it was sleeping.	When I looked at the baby, it *was not* (*wasn't*) *sleeping*.
They were singing an English song.	They *were not* (*weren't*) *singing* an English song.

Exercises

A Make these sentences **negative**. Use contracted forms.

Example: We are sitting outside the classroom.
Answer: We aren't sitting outside the classroom.

 1 We are listening to the teacher.
 2 I am writing on the blackboard. (I'm not . . .)
 3 You are learning English grammar.
 4 It is raining hard now.
 5 He is watching television.
 6 The horses are running very fast.
 7 Mark is helping his mother to cook.
 8 I am working very hard at present.
 9 Tom's sister is learning to drive a car.
10 You are singing very well today.

B In these sentences, find the verb in the **past continuous** and make it **negative**. Use contracted forms.

Example: When the train arrived, we were waiting for it.
Answer: When the train arrived, we weren't waiting for it.

1 The horses were running very fast.
2 They were pulling a very heavy load.
3 This time yesterday we were sitting here.
4 Yesterday, the snow was covering the garden.
5 It was raining hard when I came to school.
6 When I came to school, it was raining hard.
7 The boys were swimming when we saw them.
8 When we saw them, the boys were swimming.
9 You were working hard when I called.
10 When I called, you were working hard.

Lesson Eighteen

Interrogative of verbs: 'method A' – the 'peculiars'

The 'peculiars' are different from other verbs not only in the way they make their **negative**. They are different, too, in the way they make their **interrogative** or question form. They do it by **inversion**, that is by putting the 'peculiar' before its **subject**, like this:

Statement
He (**subject**) is (**verb**) a teacher.
It (**subject**) is (**verb**) ten o'clock.
His name is Ali Shah.
He can speak English.
They must go home now.
They can't understand the lesson.
He mustn't open the box.
He was here yesterday.

Question
Is (**verb**) he (**subject**) a teacher?
Is (**verb**) it (**subject**) ten o'clock?
Is his name Ali Shah?
Can he speak English?
Must they go home now?
Can't they understand the lesson?
Mustn't he open the box?
Was he here yesterday?

John could swim when he was six years old.	Could John swim when he was six years old?

Inversion of the subject and the 'peculiar' also happens when the 'peculiars' help to make a tense.

Statement	*Question*
Present continuous	
They are working hard.	Are they working hard?
Past continuous	
They were working hard.	Were they working hard?
Future	
She will help us.	Will she help us?
Present perfect	
They have finished the exercise.	Have they finished the exercise?

The 'peculiars' are the only verbs that form their interrogatives by inversion.

The way we use *have* is changing. We will explain it in Lesson 25.

Exercise

Change the following **statements** into **questions**.
Don't forget the question mark (?) at the end of your sentences.

Example: The farmer is planting rice.
Answer: Is the farmer planting rice?

1 It is six o'clock.
2 The children are in the house.
3 You can see them through the window.
4 You will come with us to the football match.
5 There are boys as well as girls in the class.
6 John is sitting in the garden.

7 His sister is with him.
8 She is helping him with his work.
9 I must do the work now.
10 Wayne is very late.
11 They are Greek children.
12 He can go now.
13 She must keep the money.
14 The clock is slow.
15 I am right.
16 My exercise is right.
17 The girls were afraid of the bull.
18 He can come here tomorrow.
19 Carl's sister was with him.
20 The children were sleeping.
21 The children are sleeping.
22 The boys were looking at the picture.
23 The boys are looking at the picture.
24 The boys can look at the picture.
25 The boys can't look at the picture.

Lesson Nineteen

Verb forms 1

When we speak of a **verb** we don't always mean just one word. A verb is rather like a family; it has several members. For example, the verb *be* has eight forms. It is a big family, the biggest of all.

Most verbs have only five members. *Give* is an example:

A	B	C	D	E
give	gives	gave	given	giving

Have has only four members:

have	has	had	(had)	having

Put has three:

put	puts	(put)	(put)	putting

JOHN: Then *put* is the same word for **present tense** and **past tense**. How do we know which it is?

TEACHER: Listen.

I went to the post office. I bought a stamp and *put* it on my letter. Then I posted it.

In that example, what tense is *put*?

JOHN: The **simple past tense**.

TEACHER: How do you know that?

Lesson Nineteen

JOHN: From the other things you said.

TEACHER: Yes. The other sentences, or the other words with it, tell us. Now look at these examples:

    1 Please buy a stamp and *put* it on the letter.

The verb *put* is a **command**. (Book 1, Lesson 10)

    2 I always *put* my books on this desk.

The verb *put* is in the **simple present tense**.

You know these things from the *context*, the other words or sentences, or from the situation.

Let's look at two other **verbs** and name the forms.

A	B	C	D	E
Base	-s form 3rd person singular present tense	Past tense	Past participle	-ing form present participle
begin come	begins comes	began came	begun come	beginning coming

D and E, the **past participle** and the *-ing* form, aren't used alone with a **subject**. We don't say or write ~~I begun last week~~ or ~~He coming here~~. But we can use D and E with 'peculiars' and a **subject**.

You will remember from Lessons 12 and 13 that we use the

'peculiar' *be* with E to make the **present continuous** and **past continuous tenses**.

He *is coming* here for tea.

She *was coming* in this direction when I saw her.

We can also use the 'peculiar' *have* (*has*) with D to make the **present perfect tense**. (See Book 3, Lesson 4)

I *have begun* to learn about participles.

She *has begun* to play tennis.

Exercises

A Try to put the forms of the verbs *give*, *speak*, *begin*, *bring*, *buy*, *write* and *work* under these headings:

A	B	C	D	E
Base	-*s* form 3rd person singular	Past tense	Past participle	-*ing* form present participle

B Give the **past participle** and the -*ing* form (**present participle**) of these **verbs**:

1 fall	5 dance	9 drink	13 take
2 know	6 cry	10 eat	14 bite
3 walk	7 try	11 forget	15 put
4 play	8 come	12 make	16 be

Lesson Twenty

Verb forms 2

Let's look at the work the different forms do.

Form	Examples	How we use the form
A Base	pull take put	1 For all the **present tense** except 3rd person singular: I/You/We/ They *pull* the rope. 2 **Commands**: *Pull* that rope. 3 With some 'peculiars': He can *pull* the rope. 4 With *to*: He tried to *pull* the rope.
B -s form	pulls takes puts	**3rd person singular, present tense** only: He/She/It/The sailor *pulls* the rope.
C Simple past tense	pulled took put	**Simple past tense**, all persons (Lesson 21): He *pulled* the rope an hour ago.
D Past participle	pulled taken put	1 With *have* for the **present perfect tense** (Book 3, Lesson 4): I *have pulled* the rope, and the flag is up. 2 With *be* for the **passive voice** (Book 3, Lesson 14): That carriage *is pulled* by two horses.

| E *-ing* form | pulling
taking
putting | 1 With *be* for the **continuous**:
He *is pulling* the rope now.
He *wasn't pulling* it an hour ago.
2 Without 'peculiars' (Book 4,
Lesson 11):
Pulling hard, they moved the
ship towards them.
Pulling ropes is hard work. |

Notice that in all the examples except those for A2
(commands) and E2 the **verb** has a **subject**. In **commands** like
A2 we 'understand' a subject:

[You] pull that rope.

and we could say:

You pull that rope! Go on!

In the E2 way of using the *-ing* form, the **subject** is not used.
It is a **non-finite** use of the *-ing* form.

A **finite verb** can be made up of one word or more . It has a
subject, and it can change for **tense** and **person**.

Exercises

A Use the same numbers (A 1, 2, 3, 4; B; C; D 1, 2; E 1, 2)
to show the use of the verb in *italics* in each of these
sentences. We give you the answers for 1 and 2.

1 The boys are *playing* football. (*Answer*: E 1)
2 The boys will *play* football this afternoon. (A 3)
3 The boys have *played* football this afternoon.
4 The boys are going to *play* football this afternoon.
5 The boys like to *play* football every afternoon.
6 I am *learning* English.
7 We are going to *learn* English.

8 Did the girls *play* tennis today?
9 Do the girls *play* tennis every day?
10 Can you *play* tennis?
11 Have you *played* tennis today?
12 Were the girls *playing* tennis today?
13 Is Richard going to *play* football today?
14 They haven't *played* tennis all afternoon.
15 They were not *playing* tennis this afternoon.

B The examples in the table use the verb *pull* and the object *the rope*. Let's repeat them here:

A1 I *pull* the rope.
  2 *Pull* that rope.
  3 He can *pull* the rope.
  4 He tried to *pull* the rope.
B He *pulls* the rope.
C He *pulled* the rope an hour ago.
D1 I *have pulled* the rope, and the flag is up.
  2 That carriage *is pulled* by two horses.
E1 He *is pulling* the rope now.
  2 *Pulling* ropes is hard work.

Now use the same numbers (omitting D2 and E2) and make sentences with the verbs *take* and *put*.

1 For the object of the verb *take*, use *a drink of water*.
  Example: A1 I take a drink of water.

2 For the object of the verb *put* use *the glass*.
  Example: A1 I put the glass on the table.

Lesson Twenty-one

Past tense and past participle: regular verbs

We have studied the **past tense** of the 'peculiars' (Lessons 10 and 11). Now let us look at the other class of verbs. Many of them form their **past tense** and **past participle** by adding *-ed*, *-d* or *-t* to the **base**. These are the **regular verbs.** Here are some of them.

Base	Simple past tense and past participle	Base	Simple past tense and past participle
walk	walked	hope	hoped
open	opened	dream	dreamed
play	played		(*or* dreamt)
want	wanted	burn	burned (*or* burnt)
dance	danced		

Note that with some verbs we double the last consonant: *stop – stopped.* Some verbs that end in *-y* change the *-y* to *-ied* (or *-id* after *a*): *cry – cried; pay – paid; lay – laid.*

The following sentences will show how we use the **simple past tense** and the **past participle**. The past participle is used with the 'peculiar' *have* to form the **present perfect tense.** (See Book 3, Lesson 4)

I *walk* (simple present tense) to school every day.

I *walked* (simple past tense) to school yesterday.

I have *walked* (past participle) to school today, and here I am.

The man *pays* (simple present tense) the workman on Saturdays.

He *paid* (simple past tense) the workman last Saturday.
He has *paid* (past participle) the workman every Saturday
for two years.

My hens *lay* (simple present tense) good eggs.
They *laid* (simple past tense) six eggs yesterday.
They have *laid* (past participle) twenty eggs since
Saturday.

As you can see from these examples, the **simple past tense**
and the **past participle** have the same form (*walked, paid,
laid*). All **regular verbs** are like this.

Exercises

A How do **regular** verbs form their **simple past tense** and
past participle?

B Give the **simple past tense** and **past participle** of each of
these **regular** verbs.

1 open	4 wash	7 cry	10 say
2 talk	5 stop	8 dry	11 lay
3 cook	6 drop	9 pay	12 dream

Past tense and past participle: irregular verbs

You have learned that a number of verbs (the **regular verbs**) make their **simple past tense** and **past participle** by adding -d, -ed or -t to their **base**. But there are a number of verbs that don't make their simple past tense and past participle like this. Instead, some of them change their vowel sound. They are the **irregular verbs**. Here are a few of the commonest irregular verbs.

Base	Simple past tense	Past participle	Base	Simple past tense	Past participle
begin	began	begun	forget	forgot	forgotten
bite	bit	bit	get	got	got
blow	blew	blown	give	gave	given
break	broke	broken	hold	held	held
bring	brought	brought	know	knew	known
buy	bought	bought	lie	lay	lain
catch	caught	caught	mistake	mistook	mistaken
come	came	come	shake	shook	shaken
draw	drew	drawn	take	took	taken
drink	drank	drunk	think	thought	thought
drive	drove	driven	throw	threw	thrown
eat	ate	eaten	wear	wore	worn
fall	fell	fallen	win	won	won
fly	flew	flown	write	wrote	written

One verb, *go,* is very irregular. It uses a different word altogether for its **past tense** – *went*; and for its **past participle** – *gone*.

Lie is rather difficult. It is an **intransitive verb**. Here are three sentences to illustrate its use.

In summer I often *lie* (simple present tense) on the shore and watch the ships sail by.

I *lay* (simple past tense) on the shore and watched them yesterday.

After I had *lain* (past participle) there for an hour, I went for a swim.

Compare this with the regular verb *lay* (see page 78). *Lay* is a **transitive verb**. *Lie* is an **intransitive verb**.

Exercises

A How do some **irregular verbs** form their **simple past tense** and **past participle**?

B Give the **simple past tense** and **past participle** of each of the verbs in the box. Arrange them in two columns, **regular verbs** in one column and **irregular verbs** in the other. We have done the first two for you.

run, jump, play, want, stop, buy, drink, eat, write, hope, cry, wear, know, burn, think, fall, come, go, lie, lay, bring.

Regular verbs			*Irregular verbs*		
jump	jumped	jumped	run	ran	run

C Change the verbs in the following sentences into the **simple past tense**. Add one of the words or phrases in the box to show past time.

> yesterday, two years ago, when I was younger, last week, last month, until yesterday, an hour ago, ten minutes ago

1 I play in the field.
2 He wants to go home.
3 The driver stops the car.
4 He drinks tea every day.
5 It begins to rain.
6 They like our house.
7 I dream every night.
8 The teacher gives me a book.
9 He sits at his desk and writes letters. (2 verbs to change)
10 Grace comes to the class early.
11 We catch fish in the river.
12 The dog eats its dinner.
13 The boys go for a holiday.
14 Richard knows Lance.
15 The plane flies very high.
16 He teaches us English.
17 I wash my hands and dry them. (2 verbs)
18 I lie in my bed.
19 He goes to school.
20 I cut the string.

D Here is a story. Rewrite it, changing all the verbs in *italics* into the **simple past tense**.

A London fog

It *is* a very foggy day in London. The fog *is* so thick that it *is* impossible to see more than a foot or so. Buses, cars and taxis *are* not able to run and *stay* by the side of the road. People *try* to find their way about on foot but they *lose* their

81

way in the fog. Mr Smith *has* a very important meeting. He *tries* to walk there but *finds* he *is* quite lost. Suddenly he *bumps* into a stranger.

'Can I help you?' the stranger *asks*.

Mr Smith *says* he *wants* to get to the Houses of Parliament.

The stranger *offers* to take him there. Mr Smith *thanks* him and they *start* to walk. The fog *gets* thicker, but the stranger *has* no difficulty in finding the way. He *goes* along one street, *turns* down another, *crosses* a square and at last they *arrive* at the Houses of Parliament. Mr Smith *can't* understand how the stranger *finds* his way.

'It is wonderful,' he *says*. 'How *do* you find the way in this fog?'

'It *is* no trouble at all to me,' *says* the stranger. 'I am blind.'

Negative of verbs:
simple present tense – 'method B'

You now know 'method A', the way we make 'peculiars' **negative**. All verbs except the 'peculiars' make their **present tense** negative by the other method, 'method B'. They do it by using *do* (*does*) and *not*. Here are some examples:

Affirmative	Negative		
		Base	
I know Harry.	I do not	know	Harry.
You know Harry.	You do not	know	Harry.
He knows Harry.	He does not	know	Harry.
We know Harry.	We do not	know	Harry.
They know Harry.	They do not	know	Harry.

There are two things that you ought to note here.

1 *Do not* is generally shortened, especially in conversation, to *don't*. *Does not* is generally shortened to *doesn't*. Here are some other examples. Compare the **affirmative** and the **negative** forms of the verb.

Affirmative	*Negative*
Richard likes ice-cream.	Richard *doesn't like* ice-cream.
Grace swims well.	Grace *doesn't swim* well.
Mary does the housework.	Mary *doesn't do* the housework.

2 Note the *s* in the third person singular.

He know*s* Harry.

There is no *s* on the *know* in the negative sentence.

He *doesn't know* Harry.

Here are some other examples:

Affirmative	*Negative*
I like learning English.	I *do not* (*don't*) *like* learning English.
We come to school on Monday.	We *do not* (*don't*) *come* to school on Sunday.
Mr Brown walks to the office.	Mr Brown *does not* (*doesn't*) *walk* to the office.
They live in Cairo.	They *do not* (*don't*) *live* in Cairo.
That bicycle costs a lot of money.	That bicycle *does not* (*doesn't*) *cost* a lot of money.
This plane flies to Kingston.	This plane *does not* (*doesn't*) *fly* to Kingston.
You know how to do this exercise.	You *do not* (*don't*) *know* how to do this exercise.
Mary works in an office.	Mary *does not* (*doesn't*) *work* in an office.

Exercises

A Give the contracted (shortened) forms of *do not* and *does not*.

B Give the **3rd person singular**, **simple present tense** of these verbs. Supply a **subject**.

Example: show
Answer: She shows

1 see	3 think	5 eat	7 learn
2 know	4 play	6 drink	8 write

C Make the **verbs** in the following sentences **negative**. (All are 'method B'.) Use the contracted forms.

Example: He likes sugar in his tea.
Answer: He doesn't like sugar in his tea.

1 I know Richard.
2 We come here every day.
3 You speak English well.
4 They live in New York.
5 He knows Richard.
6 The girl comes here every day.
7 She speaks English well.
8 Richard lives in Kingston.
9 The horse pulls the cart.
10 The horses pull the cart.
11 We swim in the river every day.
12 John swims in the river every day.
13 The bird eats the corn.
14 The birds eat the corn.
15 The cat sits on the wall.
16 The cats sit on the wall.
17 I drink tea every morning.
18 We drink tea every morning.

19 Mr Brown drinks tea every morning.
20 It rains every day.

D Make the **verbs** in the following sentences **negative**.
(Some are 'method A' and some are 'method B'.)

Example: I can see in a fog.
Answer: I can't see in a fog.

1 Carl bakes a cake.
2 Mary and Susan bake a cake.
3 Mary and Susan are baking a cake.
4 The dog chases rabbits.
5 The dogs chase rabbits.
6 The dog is chasing a rabbit.
7 The dogs are chasing a rabbit.
8 That shopkeeper sells good cakes.
9 Mary speaks English well.
10 Mary can speak English well.
11 Mary is speaking English now.
12 Harry tries to understand the lesson.
13 Harry is trying to understand the lesson.
14 The boys try to understand the lesson.
15 The boys were trying to understand the lesson.

Lesson Twenty-four

Negative of verbs:
simple past tense – 'method B'

The **simple past tense negative** of all verbs except the 'peculiars' is made by using *did* and *not* (generally shortened to *n't*) with the **base** form of the verb. Here are some examples:

Affirmative	Negative		
		Base	
I knew Harry.	I didn't	know	Harry.
You knew Harry.	You didn't	know	Harry.
He knew Harry.	He didn't	know	Harry.
We knew Harry.	We didn't	know	Harry.
They knew Harry.	They didn't	know	Harry.

Lesson Twenty-four

Affirmative	*Negative*
Mr Shah walked to the office.	Mr Shah *didn't walk* to the office.
John opened the door.	John *didn't open* the door.
They paid the money.	They *didn't pay* the money.
Mary broke the glass.	Mary *didn't break* the glass.
Louis bought a bicycle.	Louis *didn't buy* a bicycle.
I wrote a letter.	I *didn't write* a letter.

Here are some more **irregular verbs** (see page 79) with their **past tense** and **past participle**. Learn these.

Base	Past tense	Past participle
become	became	become
choose	chose	chosen
dig	dug	dug
fight	fought	fought
find	found	found
forgive	forgave	forgiven
freeze	froze	frozen
grow	grew	grown
hang	hung	hung
ride	rode	ridden
ring	rang	rung
rise	rose	risen
run	ran	run

Exercises

A Give the **simple past tense** and **past participle** of these verbs.

Example: catch
Answer: catch caught caught

1 run	5 rise	9 ring	13 ride
2 make	6 hang	10 lie	14 grow
3 become	7 choose	11 dig	15 fight
4 find	8 forgive	12 freeze	16 go

B Make the **verbs** in these sentences **negative**.

1 I made a mistake in my exercise.
2 The two boys fought in the street.
3 We rode to school on our bicycles.
4 I chose these cakes for tea.
5 The water froze in the pond last night.
6 He found the lost ball.
7 My vegetables grew very well this year.
8 The farmer dug up the potatoes.
9 Mr Brown hung the picture straight.
10 The boy rang the bell.
11 I woke very early this morning.
12 I got out of bed at six o'clock.
13 The boy ran as fast as he could.
14 John saw that picture at the cinema.
15 That baker sold us good cakes.
16 The hen laid an egg today.
17 Mary ate her breakfast quickly.
18 He went to school this morning.
19 The children sang very well.
20 We sat on these seats yesterday.

Interrogative of verbs: simple present tense – 'method B'

All verbs except the 'peculiars' form their **simple present tense interrogative** by using *do* (*does*) and the **base** form. A few examples will make this rule quite clear.

Statement	Question	Base	
I know Harry.	Do I	know	Harry?
You know Harry.	Do you	know	Harry?
He knows Harry.	Does he	know	Harry?
We know Harry.	Do we	know	Harry?
They know Harry.	Do they	know	Harry?

Statement	*Question*
You speak English.	*Do* you speak English?
	(*Do* with **base** form of *speak*)
He speaks English	*Does* he speak English?
That dog bites.	*Does* that dog bite?
	(*Does* with **base** form of *bite*)
Those dogs bite.	*Do* those dogs bite?
I speak clearly.	*Do* I speak clearly?
You come to school every day.	*Do* you come to school every day?
We sing well.	*Do* we sing well?
They play games every day.	*Do* they play games every day?
She goes swimming every week.	*Does* she go swimming every week?

Interrogative of the verb *have*

Have is still a 'method A' verb when it forms the **present perfect tense** of another verb (Book 3, Lesson 4).

  You have seen the Pyramids. (affirmative)
  Have you seen the Pyramids? (interrogative)
  He has never been to Tokyo. (affirmative)
  Has he ever been to Tokyo? (interrogative)

But *have* is changing when it means 'hold' or 'possess'. You can then treat it (in British or American English) as a 'method B' verb.

  She has a beautiful home. (affirmative)
  Does she have a beautiful home? (interrogative)
  You have a car. (affirmative)
  Do you have a car? (interrogative)

'Have you a car?' is not wrong, but it is becoming old-fashioned.

Exercise

Make the following sentences **interrogative**. Don't forget the question mark at the end of each of your questions.

Example: Uncle John takes sugar in his tea.
Answer: Does Uncle John take sugar in his tea?

1 Mary likes chocolates.
2 That baker sells good cakes.
3 I speak English well.
4 He speaks English well.
5 He takes English lessons every day.
6 Richard has a car.
7 Joyce lives in San Juan.
8 Mr Green drives to work every day.
9 The boy tries to understand the lesson.
10 The boys try to understand the lesson.
11 He writes to his brother every week.
12 They write to their brother every week.
13 You know the answer.
14 He knows the answer.
15 They learn English at school.
16 You can speak English. (Be careful! This is different and so are some that follow.)
17 The train driver sees the signal.
18 The train driver can see the signal.
19 Mary goes to school every day.
20 Mary is at school today.
21 The bird sings sweetly.
22 The bird is singing now.
23 John has a new football.
24 John carries his football on to the field.
25 John is carrying his football on to the field.

Interrogative of verbs: simple past tense – 'method B'

All verbs except the 'peculiars' make their **simple past tense interrogative** by using *did* and the **base** form. Here are some examples.

Statement	Question		
		Base	
I knew Harry.	Did I	know	Harry?
You knew Harry.	Did you	know	Harry?
He knew Harry.	Did he	know	Harry?
We knew Harry.	Did we	know	Harry?
They knew Harry.	Did they	know	Harry?

Statement	*Question*
She walked to school.	*Did* she *walk* (**base** form) to school?
He opened the door.	*Did* he *open* (**base** form) the door?
They paid the money.	Did they pay the money?
She broke the glass.	Did she break the glass?
Mrs Green drove the car.	Did Mrs Green drive the car?
Tom bought a bicycle.	Did Tom buy a bicycle?
I told you the story.	Did I tell you the story?
He came by aeroplane.	Did he come by aeroplane?
You had a car last year.	Did you have a car last year?

Here are some more **irregular verbs** with their **past tense** and **past participle**. Learn them.

Base	*Past tense*	*Past participle*
see	saw	seen
sell	sold	sold
shine	shone	shone
sing	sang	sung
sink	sank	sunk
sit	sat	sat
speak	spoke	spoken
spring	sprang	sprung
stand	stood	stood
steal	stole	stolen
stick	stuck	stuck
swim	swam	swum
teach	taught	taught
tear	tore	torn
tell	told	told
understand	understood	understood
wake	woke	woken

Exercises

A Give the **simple past tense** and **past participle** of these verbs.

Example: stick
Answer: stick stuck stuck

1 understand	5 tear	9 swim	13 speak
2 sell	6 shine	10 sink	14 stand
3 tell	7 teach	11 steal	15 wake
4 shake	8 sing	12 sit	16 spring

B Make the following sentences **interrogative**. (Don't forget the question mark.)

1 Mr Lee walked to his office.
2 The boys tried to understand the lesson.
3 He wrote to his brother every week.
4 They wrote to their brother every week.
5 The baker sold good cakes.
6 The baker burned the cakes.
7 The lesson began at nine o'clock.
8 John brought his little brother to school.
9 All the boys wore uniforms.
10 They thought carefully about that exercise.
11 John took his little brother to school.
12 His mother made a big cake for the party.
13 The ox stood in the field.
14 John held his little brother's hand.
15 Mr Green went to the office by car.
16 Fred gave his bicycle to his younger brother.
17 Henry forgot to bring his book to the class.
18 The birds flew out of the cage.
19 John's little brother came to school with him.
20 Mary had a new bicycle.